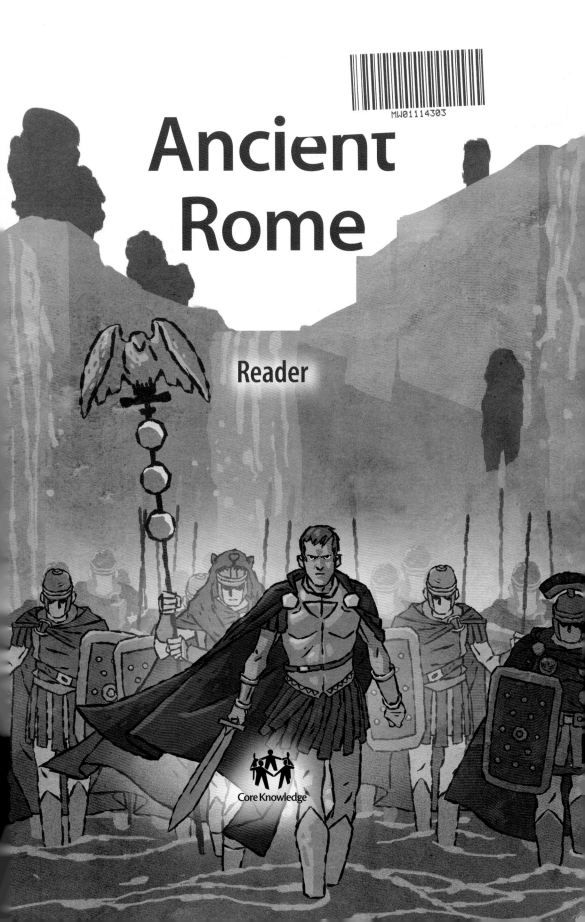

Ancient Rome

Reader

Core Knowledge

ISBN: 978-1-68380-013-2

Ancient Rome

Table of Contents

Ancient Rome
Reader
Core Knowledge History and Geography™

Chapter 1
Romulus and Remus

Now and Then Today, the city of Rome is the **capital** of a country called Italy. Two thousand years ago, Rome was the center of the world's greatest empire—the Roman Empire. The Romans ruled all the lands around the Mediterranean Sea.

How did this great empire begin? The Romans had a story, or **legend**, that explained this.

The Big Question

According to legend, how did the city of Rome begin?

Vocabulary

capital, n. the main city of a country and the home of the country's government

legend, n. an old, well-known story, usually more entertaining than truthful

In Roman legend, twins Romulus and Remus were set adrift in a basket in the Tiber River.

The Legend of Romulus and Remus

Mars, the Roman god of war, had twin sons named Romulus and Remus. When the twins were born, Mars promised that they would someday start a great empire.

A jealous uncle kidnapped the baby boys. He asked a servant to drown them in the Tiber River. The servant took pity on the boys. Instead of drowning them, he put them in a reed basket. He placed the basket in the river.

The twin boys were lucky. As the basket floated down the river, it drifted toward the riverbank. The basket hit the riverbank, and Romulus and Remus fell out. Then something moved in the bushes near the shore. It was a mother wolf! She had heard the babies crying. She nudged them with her nose and then with her paw. The wolf saw that the twins were hungry. She fed them milk just as she fed her own cubs.

In the legend, a mother wolf found Romulus and Remus.

Later, a shepherd found the boys and raised them as his own sons. After the boys grew up, they decided to build a city near the Tiber River where the wolf had found them.

The brothers began to argue. They fought over where to start building the city. During this fight, Romulus killed Remus. Romulus became the first king of the city, which would be named after him—Rome.

Romulus ruled Rome for many years, until he disappeared during a storm. The Romans believed that his father, the god Mars, took Romulus into heaven. There, Romulus became a god too.

Romulus and Remus fought over where to build their city.

The Early Years

The story of Romulus and Remus is a legend. Legends usually are not true stories. Rome was built near the Tiber River, but probably not because a wolf helped twins there. So what really happened?

Rome probably began when some farmers and shepherds built a village of small huts on one of the seven hills near the Tiber River. These people probably settled by the Tiber because it was a good place to live. The soil was rich. There was plenty of water, and the river was good for travel. An island in the river near the village made crossing the river easier.

The seven hills around the Tiber made it hard for enemies to attack. Rome grew as more people settled on those hills. That is why Rome became known as the "City of Seven Hills."

According to legend, Rome was founded in 753 BCE. The letters BCE stand for "Before the Common Era." The Common Era began when Jesus Christ was born. So Rome was founded 753 years before the birth of Jesus. That means Rome is more than 2,750 years old.

For many years, kings ruled Rome. Over time the kings became greedy for power. In 509 BCE the Romans drove out their **king**. They decided not to trust anyone else to be king. Instead, the Romans made their city a republic. In a republic, people choose **representatives** to rule for them.

Vocabulary

king, n. a male ruler who comes to power by birth and who rules for life

representative, n. a person who speaks or acts for someone else

Roman Lands, About 130 BCE

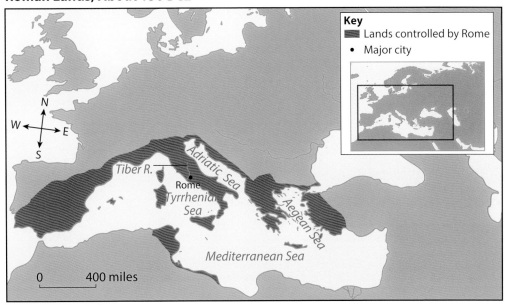

Over time, Rome came to control a large area around the Mediterranean Sea.

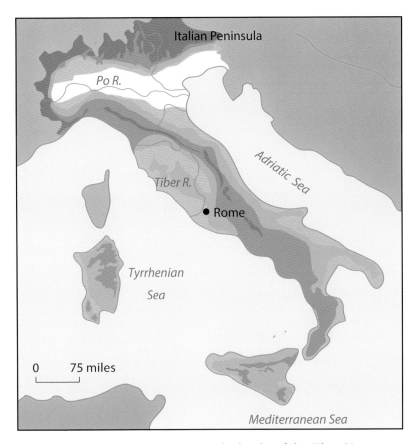

Rome became an important city on the banks of the Tiber River.

Chapter 2
Roman Gods and Goddesses

The Mighty Gods The ancient Romans believed in many **gods**. They believed that gods controlled everything in nature: the wind, sun, rain, even earthquakes.

Vocabulary

god, n. a being in the shape of a man who has the power to affect nature or people's lives

The Big Question

What does this story tell you about the importance of gods in the lives of Romans?

The Romans believed that the god Saturn controlled the harvest.

The Romans believed their gods were very involved in their lives. These gods had different names than the Greek gods because the Romans spoke Latin, a different language than the Greeks spoke. The **goddess** Juno watched over Roman brides and their marriages. The god Mars decided which side should win a battle or lose a war.

Vocabulary

goddess, n. a being in the shape of a woman who has the power to affect nature or people's lives

holy, adj. having to do with a god or religion

If a Roman farmer had a good crop, it was because the gods were pleased. If the same farmer had a bad crop, it meant the gods were angry. Because of this, the ancient Romans worried about angering their gods.

Keeping the Holy Fire Burning

Flavia was in a great hurry. She ran barefoot across the fields of her family's farm. "Please help me, Vesta," she prayed. "Let me get home before the **holy** fire goes out!"

Flavia was worried. "Why do I talk so much?" She asked herself. "Why can't I remember my job?"

Flavia and her friend Meta had spent most of the morning washing clothes in a stream. They talked as they worked.

Then Flavia remembered that she had not checked the holy fire of the goddess Vesta. She left the wet clothes with Meta and ran home as fast as she could.

Flavia's mother usually kept Vesta's fire burning. Today, though, her mother had gone to the market. At nine years old, Flavia was

The Temple of Vesta was one of the many buildings in an area of Rome called the Forum.

the oldest daughter. It became her job to keep the holy fire burning at home, just as it did in the **temple**.

The goddess Vesta watched over the **sacred** fire of every Roman home and the fire of Rome itself. The Romans did not make statues of Vesta. Fire was her only **symbol**. The Romans worshiped Vesta at every meal by throwing food into their fires.

Flavia burst into the house. She rushed to the fire. There she found just a few glowing **embers**. Quickly but carefully, she placed some straw on the embers. She blew gently to bring the flames back to life. Soon the fire burned brightly once again.

"Oh, thank you, Vesta!" Flavia cried. She placed more twigs on the burning straw. When the twigs were blazing, she put some **charcoal** in the fire. Flavia and her family believed that the smell of burning charcoal meant that Vesta was watching over the family.

Flavia and her family felt very close to Vesta and to the god Janus (/jay*nuss/), who also watched over Roman homes. Janus was a special god with two faces: one in the front of his head and one in the

This Roman coin shows the god Janus. Janus watched over doorways and archways everywhere in Rome.

back. With his two faces, Janus watched over the beginning and the end of all things. He also watched who came in and who went out of every building.

Later, Flavia again thanked the gods that the holy flame had not died out. If it had, her family would have been disgraced. She was very grateful that the gods had saved her. She promised them she would never forget again.

Chapter 3
The Roman Republic

A Boy Visits Rome Lucius (/loo*shee*us/) dressed in the dark. Almost everyone in his grandfather's villa, or country house, was asleep. Only the people who worked in the kitchen were awake. They got up early every day to prepare the morning meal.

The Big Question

In ancient Rome, what was the difference between patricians and plebeians?

Some wealthy Romans lived in beautiful country villas.

Lucius was about to try driving a **chariot**. It was a children's chariot, towed by a goat instead of a horse. Still, he was very excited.

Lucius ran barefoot over the stone floors of the villa. He carried his sandals until he reached the path through the outer garden. He put on his sandals and followed the path to a long driveway.

Simon, a Greek servant who worked for Lucius's family, waited by the chariot holding the long reins. Simon was Lucius's friend and teacher.

"Go slowly until you reach the road," Simon warned.

Lucius gripped the reins. He almost fell off when the chariot lurched forward. The chariot quickly reached full speed. Simon ran behind, shouting.

It was a wild ride. Lucius eventually got the goat under control. He was able to guide the chariot in a large circle, back to the villa. There he saw Simon, looking embarrassed. He also saw his father, looking angry.

Lucius's family

"Your mother better not hear of this, boy!" said Lucius's father. "Simon, take this goat back to the field. Lucius, go inside and find a warm cape. We go to Rome today."

"Yes, Father," said Lucius, and he ran to find his cape. Today he would ride in his father's chariot, too!

Patricians and Plebeians

Lucius was a **patrician** (/puh*trih*shun/). That meant that his family had great wealth and power. His grandfather was a Roman **senator**. His father was an army commander who had led a legion of five- to six-thousand soldiers. The family villa was surrounded by a large farm. Hundreds of enslaved people worked on this farm making olive oil and wine. Lucius's family sold the oil and wine in nearby Rome.

Only a very few Roman families were patricians. These families were very powerful. They controlled the government and the army.

What about ordinary Roman **citizens**? These people were called **plebeians** (/pleh*bee*uhnz/). Most plebeians were poor working men and women.

Early in the **republic**, the patricians had almost all of the power. They guarded their

> ### Vocabulary
>
> **patrician,** n. a member of ancient Rome's highest social class; a wealthy landowner in ancient Rome
>
> **senator,** n. a member of the Senate, the patrician lawmaking group in ancient Rome
>
> **citizen,** n. a person who belongs to a country and has protections under that country's laws
>
> **plebeian,** n. a common person without power in ancient Rome
>
> **republic,** n. a kind of government where people elect representatives to rule for them

power and gave very little to the plebeians. The plebeians could make some laws in their **assembly**, but the patrician **Senate** controlled the government. The Senate decided how government money was spent. It also decided who worked for the government and when Rome would make war and peace.

DICTATOR (IN TIMES OF WAR)

CONSULS

SENATORS

PATRICIANS

PLEBEIANS

ENSLAVED PEOPLE

Roman society was divided into different groups, with different roles and powers.

Each year two patricians were elected to serve as **consuls**. The consuls commanded the army and made sure laws were carried out. They also led meetings of the Senate.

When Rome went to war, the consuls sometimes chose a **dictator** to lead the country. The dictator had complete control over Rome. Everyone had to do what he said. The dictator's job was to make sure that Rome was safe and that the army got whatever it needed to win a war. Dictators had great power, but they were allowed to run Rome for only six months.

Vocabulary

consul, n. the most important official in the Roman Republic

dictator, n. a ruler who has total control over the country

Forum, n. the area in the center of Rome where government buildings, temples, and other important monuments were built

Lucius and his father arrived in Rome shortly after sunrise. The city was quite empty at that hour. They walked across the **Forum** in the center of Rome and found a place to sit. They watched as shops opened for the day and Romans crossed the Forum on their way to work.

Lucius Quinctius Cincinnatus

"Lucius, this great city was built by people of honor," his father said. "They served Rome because it was their duty. They wanted nothing for themselves. One of the greatest of these people was Lucius Quinctius Cincinnatus (/loo*shee*us/qwin*shee*us/sin*sih*nae*tus/). You are named for him.

"Cincinnatus had a small farm on the Tiber River not far from the city," Lucius's father continued. "One day, he was plowing his fields when messengers came to him. They asked him to go with them to the Senate. Cincinnatus was covered with dirt from his work, but he put on his toga and crossed the Tiber to Rome.

"When Cincinnatus reached the city, the senators said that he had been chosen as dictator. They told him that an enemy force had

Cincinnatus crossed the Tiber River.

trapped the entire Roman army in a mountain pass. The army would be destroyed unless help arrived soon.

"Cincinnatus ordered every shop in the city to be closed. He ordered every man and boy in the city to meet in a field with his weapons. Everyone was given a job, and soon they were ready to march. Cincinnatus led this citizen army to the rescue.

"They saved the Roman army. The next day Cincinnatus returned to the Senate. He told the senators that the army had been saved. Then he returned to his farm.

"This great Roman wanted nothing from Rome except a chance to do his duty. That is why I named you Lucius. I want you to remember your duty as a Roman."

Chapter 4
The Punic Wars

The Roman Army In its early days, Rome was a small city with a small army. This army was made up of Roman citizens and included both patricians and plebeians. It was a great honor to be in the army and defend the city of Rome.

The Big Question

What bold attack did Hannibal make in the Second Punic War?

Vocabulary

conquer, v. to win control of a land and its people by attacking an enemy or fighting a war

peninsula, n. a piece of land sticking out into a body of water, so that it is almost surrounded by water

nation, n. the land and people who live under the authority of a government and its laws; a country

The Romans fought some of their neighbors. When the Romans **conquered** an enemy, they took control of the land and people living there. In time, the Roman army became large and powerful. By the year 265 BCE, the army had conquered most of the Italian **peninsula**. In 264 BCE the Romans went to war against Carthage. Carthage was a powerful **nation** located across the Mediterranean Sea on the coast of North Africa. Today, the city of Tunis stands where Carthage once stood.

Carthage was a powerful enemy of Rome.

The Punic Wars

These wars against the Carthaginians (/kar*thuh*jin*ee*ans/) are called the Punic (/pue*nik/) Wars. The name comes from Latin, the language spoken by the Romans. The Latin word *Punicus* means Carthaginian. So, a Punic War is a war between Rome and Carthage. Since Rome and Carthage went to war three times, these wars are called the First, Second, and Third Punic Wars. They were fought between 264 and 146 BCE.

The First Punic War

The First Punic War was different from any war the Romans had fought before. Carthage was a rich nation with a large navy. When the First Punic War began, Carthage had five hundred fighting ships. Rome had no navy at all.

The Romans were determined to win. They built warships and learned to fight at sea. They learned to fight in **formation**. They trained tens of thousands of sailors to man their warships. They fought the

> **Vocabulary**
>
> **formation,** n. an orderly arrangement, such as in rows or a line

Carthaginians for twenty-three long years. When the First Punic War ended in 241 BCE, the Romans had won.

Hannibal

At the end of the First Punic War, a young Carthaginian boy named Hannibal waited for his father to return from battle. His father was an important leader in the Carthaginian army. Hannibal wanted to be a soldier like his father. More than anything, he wanted to fight against the Romans.

When Hannibal's father returned, he became commander of Carthage's army. He then conquered the rich lands along the

Roman soldiers trained to fight in formation.

northwest coast of the Mediterranean. Today this area is called Spain.

When he was nine years old, Hannibal went to Spain with his father and the army. Hannibal grew to be an excellent soldier, like his father. When he was twenty-six years old, Hannibal took command of the Carthaginian army.

Hannibal was a great general. He was brave and clever in battle. He treated his men fairly and earned their respect and loyalty.

The Second Punic War

Hannibal still wanted to fight Rome. In 219 BCE he attacked a town that was friendly with Rome. This attack started the Second Punic War.

Next, Hannibal decided to march his army from Spain to Italy. This meant crossing wide rivers and the tall snow-covered mountains known as the Alps.

It would be hard for the soldiers to cross these rivers and mountains. Hannibal also had to get thousands of horses and

Hannibal's Route to Roman Lands

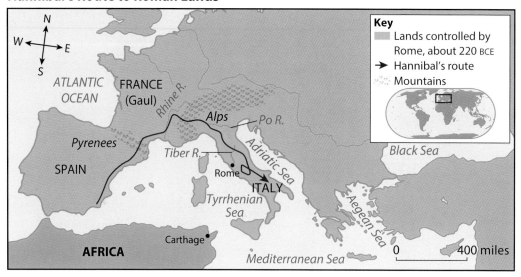

Hannibal's route from Spain to the lands of Rome

dozens of elephants across these **barriers**. The Carthaginian army used African elephants in battle. Most of their enemies in Europe had never seen elephants and were terrified by them.

The Romans thought that no army would ever be able to cross the rugged Alps. They were wrong. The Carthaginians made it over the Alps and onto the Italian peninsula. The crossing took fifteen hard days, and Hannibal lost almost half his men.

Hannibal fought the Romans on the Italian peninsula for the next sixteen years. He won great battles, but Romans would not give up.

Eventually, the Romans sent an army to attack Carthage. Hannibal rushed home. Outside Carthage, Hannibal met a Roman army led by General Scipio Africanus (/sip*ee*oeh/af*rih*kay*nus/). The Roman army won the battle. Carthage surrendered, but Hannibal

Roman legions feared the elephants when they first saw them.

continued to fight. He moved from place to place, staying away from the Romans. When the Romans finally trapped him, Hannibal refused to surrender. Instead, he killed himself.

The Third Punic War

After the Second Punic War, Rome and Carthage were at peace for more than fifty years. Then in 149 BCE, the Third Punic War began. The Romans sent a huge army to Africa. The fighting lasted only three years. In the end, the Romans destroyed the city of Carthage. The Carthaginians who were not killed were enslaved.

Chapter 5
Julius Caesar

The Roman Army The Romans were great conquerors. They had large, well-trained armies. Their navy ruled the seas. After the Romans defeated an enemy, the captured land became part of Rome.

The Big Question

Why did some Romans think Julius Caesar was a hero?

These lands were called **provinces**. The Roman Senate sent a **governor** to each province. The governor made sure the province paid **taxes** to Rome. The Romans usually let the conquered people keep their laws and customs. Sometimes they even made the conquered people citizens of Rome.

The Romans conquered lands that once were part of ancient Greece. They brought many Greek statues and paintings back to Rome. They also brought Greek stories and plays and copied Greek building styles.

The Impact of Ancient Greece

The Romans copied the Greeks because they admired the beauty of Greek art, writings, and buildings. Wealthy Romans kept enslaved Greek servants who had once been teachers

The columns of the Roman Temple of Saturn were copied from Greek architecture.

and doctors. Many Romans learned the Greek language.

Trouble in the Republic

As Roman armies conquered more lands, the wealthiest Romans grew richer. They used enslaved people to work on their land. Enslaved people were not paid for the work they did, such as farming. As a result, rich farmers could sell their crops for less money than farmers who had to pay workers. This gave richer farmers a big advantage over other farmers. Many poor farmers were forced out of business and lost their land.

Many farmers who lost their land came to Rome. They were out of work and hungry. They wanted help from the Roman government. But the Senate controlled the government, and many senators were rich landowners. They did not care about helping the poor people of Rome.

Several leaders told the Senate to help the people who had lost their land. But the Senate did not listen.

Unhappiness among the Roman people grew. The Roman Republic was growing weak. In its final days, one man took control of the government. His name was Julius Caesar (/jool*yus/see*zur/).

Julius Caesar

Julius Caesar was born in 100 BCE. Although his parents were patricians, they were not very wealthy. Caesar knew he would have to work hard to get ahead. As a young boy, he did well in his studies. He also did well at sports, especially horseback riding.

Caesar served in the Roman army in Asia. When he returned to Rome, he worked as a lawyer. He made friends with many people in the Roman government.

Caesar was a great speaker and was chosen for several government jobs. One of his jobs was to manage the games and shows for the city of Rome. These shows helped amuse and entertain the people of Rome. Caesar borrowed money from his wealthy friends. He used the money to make the greatest games and shows in Roman history. His games made Caesar popular with the people of Rome.

Even as a young man, Julius Caesar had achieved many things.

Caesar became friends with powerful leaders in the Senate and in the army. One of these friends was

Pompey (/pahm*pee/), Rome's most famous general. Caesar also had enemies in the Senate, especially among the wealthy landowners.

Caesar was elected consul in 59 BCE. Then he became governor of two provinces next to an area called Gaul. Today we know this area as southern France and northern Italy.

Julius Caesar was honored for this bravery.

Caesar led a large Roman army into Gaul. The Gauls were fierce warriors, but Caesar was an excellent general. His soldiers loved him. Caesar won many victories. His conquests in the Gallic Wars of 58–51 BCE made him a hero to many Romans.

Crossing the Rubicon

Caesar's old friend Pompey became jealous of Caesar. He watched Caesar grow more powerful with each victory. Soon Pompey was no longer Rome's most famous general. Caesar was.

Pompey joined Caesar's enemies in the Senate. They hated and feared Caesar. They thought he was too popular with the Roman people. His army had grown too powerful. The Senate ordered Caesar to give up his army and return to Rome.

> **Vocabulary**
>
> **border,** n. an imaginary line that marks the edge of a country or other piece of land

Caesar faced a hard choice. He led his army to the Rubicon (/roo*bih*kahn/) River, which was the **border** between Gaul and Italy. Caesar stopped and thought about what to do next.

If his army crossed the Rubicon, he would be at war with Rome. But if he left his army in Gaul, he would have no protection

Vocabulary

civil war, n. a war between people who live in the same country

against his enemies. They would probably kill him. Caesar decided to fight. He led his army across the river and started a **civil war**.

Civil War

The war did not go well for Caesar's enemies. Caesar drove them out of Italy into Spain and finally to Greece. There, Caesar won a clear victory. After he won, Caesar forgave the senators who fought against him.

Caesar's old friend Pompey escaped. He went to Egypt, where the king had him killed. For the king, this proved to be a terrible mistake.

Caesar crossed the Rubicon River and started a civil war in Rome.

Chapter 6
Cleopatra, Queen of Egypt

Arrival in Egypt In 48 BCE Julius Caesar sailed along the Nile River and arrived in Alexandria, Egypt, with a small group of soldiers. Caesar was looking for Pompey. He went to the king's palace. There he learned that Pompey was dead.

The Big Question

What did Julius Caesar do in order to protect Cleopatra?

The king of Egypt had trusted his advisers. They had promised him that Caesar would be happy that Pompey was dead. They were wrong. Pompey was a Roman general. Caesar saw Pompey's murder as an insult to Rome.

Cleopatra

While Caesar was still a guest at the palace, a servant entered carrying a large, rolled-up rug. Caesar watched as the rug was unrolled. Cleopatra (/klee*oe*pat*ruh/), the queen of Eygpt, was hiding inside.

Cleopatra begged Caesar to protect her from her brother, the king. She said the king and his advisers were planning to murder her.

It took a little while for Caesar to reply. He stared at Cleopatra and listened to her voice. He would certainly protect her. He wanted to keep the beautiful queen near. Cleopatra stayed with Caesar.

Notice Cleopatra's clothing and jewelry in this carving.

The king and his advisers were angry that Cleopatra had outsmarted them. They were also angry that Caesar agreed to protect Cleopatra. They ordered the Egyptian army to surround the palace. They thought this would make Caesar change his mind. Once again, they were wrong.

Caesar ordered the Roman army in nearby Syria to march on Alexandria. Caesar killed the king's chief adviser. The Egyptian king fled from his own palace. When the Roman army arrived, Caesar took command. He easily defeated the Egyptian army. The king of Egypt died in the battle.

Cleopatra was very grateful to Caesar. She asked him to travel through Egypt with her. According to legend, they sailed up the Nile River on her royal **barge**. Caesar learned a lot about Cleopatra on this journey.

Cleopatra was actually Greek, not Egyptian. Almost three hundred years earlier, the Greek king Alexander the Great had conquered

Cleopatra ruled over a rich kingdom.

Egypt and built the great city of Alexandria. Cleopatra was a **descendant** of one of Alexander's Greek generals.

Vocabulary

descendant, n. someone who is related to a person or group of people who lived in the past

Cleopatra studied hard to be a good ruler. She learned about other countries from people who came to study in Alexandria's great library. She also learned to speak many languages. She was the only one in the history of her royal family who could speak to the Egyptian people in their own language.

Caesar came to trust Cleopatra. He did not want to make Egypt a Roman province. He wanted Cleopatra to remain queen of Egypt. Caesar also fell in love with Cleopatra.

Caesar, however, was a busy man. He left Egypt to finish the war against Pompey's remaining army.

Caesar was a mighty leader.

Chapter 7
Julius Caesar Dies

More conquests Julius Caesar continued to conquer. When he left Egypt, he led his army to Asia Minor, the home of modern-day Turkey. There, Caesar once again showed he was a great general.

The Big Question

What were the reasons behind the actions taken against Julius Caesar and Marc Antony?

Caesar sent a message to the Senate about his latest conquest. It was only three Latin words: "*Veni, vidi, vici*" (/vee*nee/vee*dee/vee*kee/). The words mean, "I came, I saw, I conquered."

Next, Caesar went to North Africa and won another victory. Then, he went to Spain and defeated armies led by Pompey's sons. Finally, he returned to Rome. There he became dictator—for life. Caesar was now the most powerful man in the world.

Caesar changed the Roman government. He lowered taxes, appointed new senators, and replaced several greedy governors in the provinces. He gave land to Roman soldiers and food to the poor.

Caesar's enemies in the Senate did not like these changes. They thought Caesar was acting like a king and had too much power.

Caesar wrote about his victories.

Caesar invited Cleopatra to Rome to celebrate his victories. He gave her gifts and placed a statue of her in a temple.

Caesar's enemies worried that Caesar would marry Cleopatra and move the government to Alexandria. They also disliked the way Caesar had ended the republic and set himself up as a dictator for life. They decided to **assassinate** Caesar.

The Assassination

The Romans called March 15 the Ides of March. On that day in 44 BCE, several of Caesar's enemies entered the Senate with knives hidden under their **togas**.

When Caesar entered the Senate, his enemies stabbed him. One of the attackers was Brutus (/broo*tus/), a man Caesar had forgiven after the civil war. Caesar thought Brutus was his friend. Surprised that Brutus had joined his enemies, Caesar's last words were, "Et tu, Brute?" (/et/too/broo*tay/). This means "You too, Brutus?"

The murder of Caesar

Marc Antony and Octavian

After Caesar died, another civil war began. On one side were Brutus and the others who supported the killing of Caesar. On the other side were Caesar's supporters. In 42 BCE Caesar's friends won the war. The leaders of this group were Marc Antony and Octavian.

Marc Antony was a famous general. He wore a thick cape that looked like a lion's skin. He told his soldiers that he was related to the legendary hero Hercules. Hercules had killed a mighty lion and worn its skin as a cape. Antony's soldiers respected his courage in battle, but Antony liked to brag. He could also be careless.

Marc Antony shared control of the government with Caesar's adopted son, Octavian (/ahk*tay*vee*un/). Octavian called himself "the young Caesar." He was eighteen years old when Caesar died. Octavian was the opposite of Antony. He was proper in his dress and manner. He was also careful about his decisions.

Antony Vs. Octavian: The Roman Empire After the Death of Julius Caesar

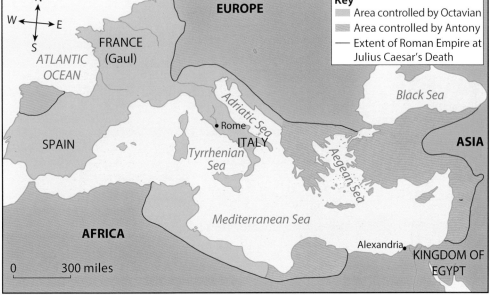

After Caesar's death, Antony and Octavian fought for control of the empire.

Antony and Octavian each took part of the **empire** to command. Octavian's part was in the west, near Spain. Antony's part was in the east, near Egypt.

Antony and Cleopatra

Antony wanted to conquer more lands, but he needed money for his army. He asked Cleopatra to exchange the riches of Egypt for his protection. Cleopatra agreed. She invited Antony to stay with her in Egypt. The two fell in love.

Then Antony's wife died. Though he was free to marry Cleopatra, Antony would not. He knew that many Romans did not trust Cleopatra. She was too clever, too rich, and too powerful. She was also a **foreigner**.

Antony left Cleopatra, returned to Rome, and married Octavian's sister, Octavia. He knew that important Romans would approve of this marriage. He also believed the marriage would help him keep the peace with Octavian. Still, Antony returned to the east three years later. He went back to his wars of conquest—and to Cleopatra.

> **Vocabulary**
>
> **empire,** n. a group of countries or territories under the control of one government or one ruler
>
> **foreigner,** n. someone from another country

Antony and Cleopatra fell in love.

Things went badly for Antony. He lost half his army and conquered nothing. The army needed food, clothing, and weapons.

Octavia wanted to help her husband. She loaded ships with **supplies** and sailed to the east. Despite this help, Antony ordered Octavia back to Rome. He made it clear that he preferred Cleopatra to his **noble** Roman wife.

Vocabulary

supplies, n. food and other goods that are needed for a certain purpose

noble, adj. belonging to the highest social class

Octavian was angry. Antony had insulted his sister. Octavian spoke out against Antony and Cleopatra. He said they were planning to take control of the entire Roman world.

Octavian prepared for war. As always, he was careful. He asked Agrippa, Rome's most famous naval commander, to help.

Octavian attacked first. Agrippa trapped Antony and Cleopatra and forced them to fight at sea. They were no match for Agrippa. After their defeat in the Battle of Actium (31 BCE), Antony and Cleopatra escaped to Egypt.

The end came quickly. Antony's army surrendered. Antony killed himself. Cleopatra knew that Octavian would bring her back to Rome in chains. She dressed in her most beautiful costume and held a deadly snake to her skin. When Octavian's guards found her, Cleopatra appeared to be asleep, but she was dead.

Chapter 8
Caesar Augustus

The Big Question

What were some of Caesar Augustus's many accomplishments?

Octavian's Return When Octavian returned to Rome, he was thirty-three years old. Up to that time he had had a remarkable life. He had been adopted by Julius Caesar as a boy. Then he was named consul of Rome when he was only nineteen years old.

Octavian and Marc Antony had beaten Caesar's enemies. Each had taken a part of the Roman Empire to command. Then Octavian beat Antony and Cleopatra. He conquered Egypt and took Cleopatra's wealth for himself. He also had 280,000 soldiers in his army.

This was just the beginning. Now Octavian was ready to begin the most important part of his life. He was ready now to become ruler of Rome. In this role, Octavian would show himself to be a smart leader who used good sense.

At 33, Octavian was ready to become ruler of Rome.

Closing the Doors of War

Octavian showed his smart leadership shortly after he returned from Egypt. At that time, the Roman people were celebrating Octavian's victory, which ended the civil war and saved Rome. Octavian led a crowd to the temple of Janus. The temple's gates were left open during times of war. They were closed during peacetime. Rome had almost always been at war, so the gates had rarely been closed.

Octavian closed the gates. This act showed the Roman people they would now live in peace. Octavian then set out to fulfill this promise.

Soon afterward, Octavian bought land for his soldiers. He told them it was time to leave the army and go back to being farmers.

Octavian himself went back to his job as consul. He was reelected three years in a row. Then he told the Senate he wanted to give back all his power. He would serve Rome in any way the Senate decided.

Octavian Becomes Augustus

The Senate decided that Octavian should command the armies in all the large provinces. They also decided that Octavian should have a new name. He was to be called Caesar Augustus (/awe*gus*tus/). *Augustus* is a Latin word that means revered one. To be revered is to be the most admired and respected.

Augustus was named the First Citizen of Rome, and the month of his birth was renamed for him. Today, we call that month August. (July had already been named for Julius Caesar.)

Augustus was not a king or a dictator. All his power came from the Senate. He was always respectful of the senators and the assemblies. The senators trusted Augustus because he used his power wisely.

Augustus used his power to name new governors for the provinces and new senators. He also made changes in the Roman army. He paid soldiers more money. This helped make the army a good place for poor men to earn a living.

Augustus built good roads throughout the Roman Empire. These roads connected Rome and the provinces. Augustus often visited the provinces to check if the governors were doing a good job.

Augustus Rebuilds Rome

At the end of the civil war, Rome was a dirty, overcrowded city. Most of the streets and buildings needed repair. The **aqueducts**, which carried water to the city, were also crumbling.

Many people who had lost their land during the civil war now lived in Rome. They were poor and hungry. They lived in old buildings that often caught fire or collapsed.

Augustus led Rome to new heights of glory.

Augustus bought food for the poor. He rebuilt many old buildings. He made laws to require that all buildings met safety standards. He started Rome's first fire and police departments. He put Agrippa, his naval commander, in charge of the city's water supply. Agrippa and his forces rebuilt the old aqueducts.

Augustus wanted everyone to know about the citizens who had helped to make Rome great. He built a beautiful new Forum in Rome. Around this new Forum, he placed statues of Roman heroes.

Augustus filled the city with beautiful new buildings. He built theaters, meeting places, and a grand new Senate building. He changed Rome from a dirty, ugly place to one of the most beautiful cities in the world.

Augustus also helped make Roman religion stronger. He repaired Rome's old temples and built new ones. He brought back many old **religious ceremonies** and festivals.

Augustus loved books and ideas. He often visited with writers and poets to listen as they read their

The beautiful Pantheon was used to worship all of the Roman gods. The original Pantheon was built by Agrippa during the rule of Augustus.

work aloud. He asked wealthy Romans to be **patrons** to writers. These patrons gave money to writers so they could keep writing. During the time of Augustus, talented writers wrote many great works. People today still read some of these great works.

Rome's First Emperor

Rome honored Augustus for rebuilding the city and making life better for the people. They named him "Father of His Country." Later, he was called Rome's first **emperor**.

Augustus was the most powerful man in the world, yet he lived simply. His house was small. His meals were plain. He was loyal to his wife and family and the Roman people.

Augustus ruled as emperor from 27 BCE until 14 CE. The letters *CE* stand for the phrase *Common Era*. The Common Era began with the birth of Jesus. So, Augustus ruled until fourteen years after the birth of Jesus.

Caesar Augustus had a long and successful rule.

Chapter 9
Roman Lands

The Roman World Once, it was very easy to see all of the Roman world from one spot. In 750 BCE, all you had to do was climb a hill near the Tiber River. From that place you could see a few farms, fishermen's huts, and small clusters of houses. That was all there was to Rome at that point in history.

The Big Question

How did the Mediterranean Sea and Roman roads help the Romans manage their empire?

In time, the Roman world grew. As you know from reading earlier chapters, the Romans were good at conquering other lands. They were also good at ruling the lands they conquered. The Romans expected conquered people to work hard and send taxes to Rome.

Eventually, the Roman world grew so large that the only way to see the whole empire would have been to look down from space. Of course, there was no way to do that in Roman times. Instead, the Romans used maps to show all the lands they ruled. These lands were located on three **continents**: Europe, Asia, and Africa.

Vocabulary

continent, n. one of the seven large land areas on Earth

Rome began as a small village on the Tiber River.

The Roman Empire, 117 CE

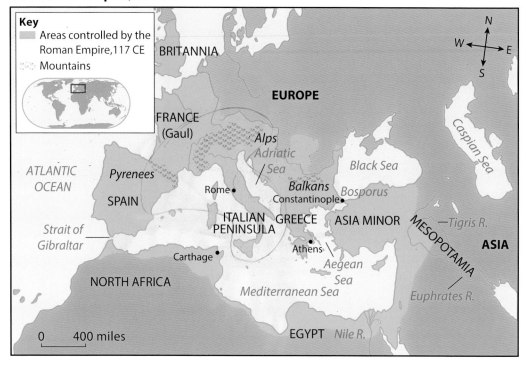

Rome's empire spread from the Italian peninsula through most of Europe and parts of Asia and Africa.

The map shows the Roman Empire when it was very large. Let's take a tour.

Italy and the Mediterranean

The city of Rome is located on the Italian peninsula. Do you see it? If you can't find the Italian peninsula, look for the piece of land that looks like a boot. Do you see the toe and the high heel?

The Italian peninsula is part of the continent of Europe. Between the Italian peninsula and the rest of Europe are the Alps. The Alps are a high snow-covered **mountain range.** Hannibal and his elephants crossed the Alps during the Second Punic War.

> ### Vocabulary
>
> **mountain range,** n. a line of mountains

The Italian peninsula sticks out into the Mediterranean Sea. Once the Romans controlled the Italian peninsula, they conquered islands and coastal areas around the Mediterranean. After a while, the Romans controlled the whole Mediterranean region. They called the Mediterranean "our sea."

Greece and the Balkans

The Adriatic Sea is northeast of the Italian peninsula. Across the Adriatic Sea is Greece. As you know, ancient Greece was very important to the Romans. The Romans liked Greek ideas about education, art, building, and government. They used these ideas in Rome. They also brought these ideas to their provinces.

East of Greece is the Aegean Sea. The Aegean is connected to another large body of water: the Black Sea. These two seas are connected by a narrow waterway, or **strait**. This strait is called the Bosporus. It separates Europe from Asia Minor.

> **Vocabulary**
>
> **strait,** n. a narrow body of water that connects two large bodies of water

The Bosporus passes through a city that was once called Constantinople. Today its name is Istanbul. This city was important to the Roman Empire. You will learn more about it later.

Asia and Africa

Constantinople is on the tip of the peninsula called Asia Minor. Today the peninsula is home to the nation of Turkey. Two thousand years ago, Asia Minor was part of the Roman Empire. It is from this place that Julius Caesar sent his famous "Veni, vidi, vici" message.

The Romans also controlled Mesopotamia and the **kingdom** of Egypt. Egypt was the home of Cleopatra. It was also one of the richest of Rome's provinces. It had ports on the Mediterranean Sea and the Red Sea. It also had rich lands along the Nile River.

The remains of the Library of Celsus in Ephesus, Turkey, are what is left of this ancient Roman building.

The Romans had provinces along the North African coast too. Carthage controlled some of that coastline until the end of the Third Punic War. Then Rome gained control of this land.

Vocabulary

kingdom, n. a country ruled by a king or queen

Back to Europe

At the western end of the North African coastline is the Strait of Gibraltar. This strait connects the Mediterranean Sea and the Atlantic Ocean. Spain is north of Gibraltar, on the continent of Europe. The Romans conquered Spain. Then, Julius Caesar conquered the large area to the north. The Romans called this area Gaul. Today, we call this area France.

The Romans also had an island province north of Europe. They called this province Britannia. Today this land is part of Great Britain.

All Roads Lead to Rome

To control such a large empire, Roman officials needed a way to travel easily. To do this, they built roads. These roads were paved with smooth slabs of stone. The Roman army could travel quickly over the paving stones to get where it was needed.

The Appian Way, the most famous road of ancient Rome, was built in 312 BCE. Parts of the road are still used today.

The Roman Empire had more than fifty thousand miles of roads. These roads connected every province of the empire to Rome itself. That is why the Romans said, "All roads lead to Rome."

Today, in areas of Asia, Africa, and Europe, some highways and railroad lines still follow the routes of the ancient Roman roads.

Chapter 10
Roads, Bridges, and Aqueducts

Grandfather's Traveling School

One morning in 100 CE, a Roman patrician named Marcus heard the slap of small sandals on the stone floor of his villa. Marcus wondered which of his children was up so early.

The Big Question

How did Roman engineering skills help the Roman Empire become so successful?

Vocabulary

scroll, n. a roll of paper or other material with written information

The slapping sound grew louder. Then Marcus saw Linus, his seven-year-old son, carrying a great armload of **scrolls**. At that moment, the footsteps were interrupted by an awful crash. Then came the sound of heavy scrolls bouncing and rolling on the smooth stone floor.

Marcus hurried into the hall. Linus was trying to gather up the scrolls. Lucia, Linus's eleven-year-old sister, was shaking her head and scolding her brother.

The Romans used scrolls to record written information—such as this saying, which means "Let us therefore rejoice while we are young."

"Now you have woken Father. Why can't you be careful? Next you will wake Grandfather."

She was right. Grandfather was awake. And he had a message for his grandson.

"You won't find answers in those scrolls, boy. You and your sister have a lot to learn. You won't learn it crawling around my villa in the dark. Tell Nikos, your teacher, that we are going to Rome. But first, I'll have a word with your father."

Marcus smiled at his father as the older man led them outside.

"Marcus, my grandchildren have been in the countryside too long. I asked them some questions yesterday. They know almost nothing about Rome. They have never even seen an aqueduct! It

Linus and Lucia are going to learn about Rome.

is time they learned. As head of the family, I'm going to see to it. They will be in my traveling school beginning today."

Marcus was grateful to his father, who was a Roman senator. Linus and Lucia were getting a wonderful gift.

Linus and Lucia climbed aboard a large wagon. Nikos, the teacher, was next. They were followed by two servants, who would cook meals and care for the horses.

The senator wore a purple-trimmed toga and rode a beautiful black horse. He waved good-bye to Marcus and rode away, followed by his guards and the heavy wagon.

Road Building

"Linus and Lucia, you are going to learn how to build a road," said Grandfather. "Climb down. We'll walk from here."

The group walked toward a cloud of dust in the distance. As they neared the dust cloud, they saw hundreds of men digging and carrying stones.

Their grandfather explained: "First these men dig a trench, which is a big hole in the ground. They fill the trench with large stones and **gravel**. Then they lay down smooth slabs of stone to make the road's **surface**. They also make the road a little higher in the middle. That way, the rain will flow off it.

> **Vocabulary**
>
> **gravel,** n. tiny stones used to make paths or to make concrete
>
> **surface** n., the top layer

"Nikos will show you a map of the Roman roads, which connect all the Roman provinces. These fine roads are one of our most valuable treasures.

"Next," Grandfather continued, "we're going to see where this road is going. We will have a good view from that hilltop."

Bridge Building

The view was very good indeed. The road was headed across a broad **valley** toward a wide river. Hundreds of men were building a bridge across the river.

Again, the senator explained how it was done. "First, they line two boats up side by side. Then they build a wooden platform across them. They add more boats and make the platform longer until it stretches all the way across the river.

"When the long platform is finished, they build underwater **pillars**. These support the bridge."

"How do they build the pillars?" the children asked.

"They pound a wooden **stake** into the bottom of the river," the older man explained. "Then they put another stake next to it, and another, until they make a circle of stakes. They pull chains around the stakes to make the circle very tight. That way, no water can leak in between the stakes.

"When the chains are tight, they empty out the water inside the circle. Then they build a stone pillar inside the circle of stakes. They build all the pillars the same height. Then they connect them with wooden **arches**.

> ### Vocabulary
>
> **valley,** n. a low area of land surrounded by higher ground, such as hills or mountains
>
> **pillar,** n. a tall, solid support post
>
> **stake,** n. a thin, pointed post
>
> **arch,** n. a curved structure that has an opening below and that supports something above

"Next they build another platform over the arches. Then they replace the wooden arches and the wooden platform with stone to finish the bridge. The stone bridge will be strong enough to hold a Roman army legion."

Aqueducts

"What is that?" Lucia asked. "It looks like a bridge, but it is so much larger and so high in the air. What is it, Grandfather?"

"It is an aqueduct. It carries water from the mountain lakes to the city of Rome. The aqueduct is a great pipe that carries water high over valleys and hillsides," Grandfather replied.

"Aqueducts are built like bridges. Arches of stone connect stone support pillars. The great pipe lies on top of the arches the way the road lies on the arches of the bridge," he continued.

The two children stared in wonder.

Magnificent Roman aqueducts can still be seen today.

Chapter 11
The Buildings of Rome

A Visit to Rome Nikos smiled as he lifted the heavy scroll back into its case. Linus and Lucia had spent many hours studying the map of Roman roads. Their grandfather asked some hard questions about the map. Linus and Lucia knew every answer.

The Big Question

How was Rome similar to a modern city?

That night they traveled to Rome. The smooth paved road shone in the moonlight. The senator and his guards rode close to the wagon. The clopping sounds of the horses' hooves filled the cool night air.

When they reached Rome, its narrow streets were crowded with wagons. Although many Romans stayed in at night, food and supplies for the morning arrived while they slept.

They passed through noisy, crowded neighborhoods filled with apartment houses. The city grew quieter as they rode into the senator's neighborhood. Once they went through his house gates, the senator's gardens were as quiet as his country villa.

Servants with torches ran into the yard. They unloaded the wagon and led the horses to the stables. The children followed their grandfather into the house. Nikos followed with his case of scrolls.

Rome's neighborhoods were filled with apartment houses.

"Nikos, come and have something to eat," said the senator. "The children did well with their lessons.

"Tomorrow I want to take Linus to the market in the Forum. That boy thinks Rome is nothing but chariot races and **gladiators**. I want him to learn about life in our city. He will find plenty of life in the Forum."

The Temple of Jupiter

The next morning, Lucia woke up in a strange room. For a moment, she forgot she was in her grandfather's house in Rome. Then she jumped out of bed. Last night, Grandfather promised a surprise if she got up early.

Lucia found him waiting near a stairway. The senator led the way up the stairs to the roof. Lucia took his hand as they climbed. When she looked up, she saw a strange light above the house. When they reached the top of the stairs, Lucia saw the source of the glowing light.

The first faint light of dawn had just reached a nearby hilltop. There, a huge white building glowed in the early light. On its roof stood a huge statue of a bearded man driving a chariot pulled by four great horses.

Temple of Jupiter

Grand pillars of pure white **marble** surrounded the entire building. Lucia had never seen anything as beautiful.

"There is the greatest symbol of Rome, the Temple of Jupiter," Grandfather said. "Today we will visit that temple, just the two of us. Linus will go with Nikos to explore the marketplace."

Lucia looked down at the senator's gardens. The first birds began to sing. She saw Nikos and Linus leaving the house on their way to the marketplace.

The Marketplace

"Nikos, are you sure we will see fish bigger than me?" asked Linus.

"Yes, Linus, and fish smaller than your fingers. We will see every fish in the sea and maybe even an octopus. But we must hurry," said Nikos.

Before long Linus was staring, wide-eyed, at the fish being sold in the market. Hundreds of people were carrying fish, smelling fish, and poking fish with their fingers. Some fish were so large that two men could barely carry them.

Some were so small that a hundred fit in a basket.

Most of the fish went to small food stands. Few Romans had kitchens at home. Almost everyone in Rome bought meals cooked at food stands.

Nikos and Linus left the fish sellers and went to the meat, grain, oil, wine, and spice sellers. Linus saw how Rome brought food to the one million or so people who lived there. By the end of the day, he had learned some very important things. He was also very hungry.

A Busy City

Lucia and her grandfather climbed the white marble steps of the Temple of Jupiter. A huge gold statue of the king of the gods looked down on them as they entered.

Grandfather stopped to speak to another senator. Lucia waited on the steps of the temple. She looked out over the city. Rome was so big! The people looked tiny as they walked among the great buildings.

Lucia turned her eyes on the Forum of Rome. Thousands of people were talking and shouting, buying and selling, walking, running, and standing still. The Forum was like the city—filled with noise and excitement and people.

The city of Rome was a busy place full of interesting sights.

Lucia and Grandfather walked all through Rome that day. They visited temples and theaters. They ate at food stands and drank from the fountains. They even saw animals being led across the city.

Grandfather pointed out people from every province. There were Egyptians, Greeks, redheaded people from Gaul, and dark-skinned people from Africa.

Lucia was happy to be part of this noisy, crowded, exciting city. There was so much to see and to learn.

"Grandfather, will you take me again tomorrow? Please? I want to know more of our city. I am so proud to be a Roman!"

Chapter 12
Gladiators and Chariot Races

Linus Gets Lost "It appears my grandson has a poor memory," said Grandfather. "I told him not to go into the underground passageway. Yet that is exactly where he has gone."

Vocabulary

Colosseum, n. a large stadium in ancient Rome

Lucia started down the passageway to the underground part of the **Colosseum**. She thought maybe she could help find Linus, even though she did not like the look of the dark passageway.

Grandfather called her back. "No, Lucia. Don't you go looking for your brother," he said. "I will speak to the commander of the sailors. We may need some help to find him down there. Until then, Linus can learn just how lost he can get. Perhaps it will help his poor memory."

Grandfather turned to Nikos. "Tell the commander of the sailors I want to see him."

Many Romans enjoyed watching spectacular events at the Colosseum.

Nikos began climbing the hundreds of steps to the top of the Colosseum. The senator took Lucia's hand and led her onto the sunlit floor of the Colosseum.

"Lucia, I want you to understand how they built this great **arena**," said Grandfather. "It is the finest in Rome. It has seating for fifty thousand people. The round outside wall is built like an aqueduct, with arches of stone stacked on each other. Arches also support the inside rows of seats, which look like a giant oval stairway.

> ### Vocabulary
>
> **arena,** n. an area surrounded by seating for the public, where sports events are held
>
> **chamber,** n. a small space or room

"Look all around the top of the arena. There are one thousand sailors from the Roman navy up there. They are waiting for the command to roll out the awning. The awning is a giant canvas roof that shades the seats from the sun.

"There are many passageways under the floor of the arena. They connect dozens of **chambers**. Some of these rooms hold wild animals. Others are for the gladiators. One passageway connects the gladiator school to the arena. When it is time for a big gladiator fight, the gladiators are led out of one door, and the animals out of another."

Linus Meets the Gladiators

Linus was very sure of two things. He was very sure he was lost. He was also very sure that he wanted to get out of the underground passages.

Just then, he heard a low growling sound. It was a sound that a large animal might make.

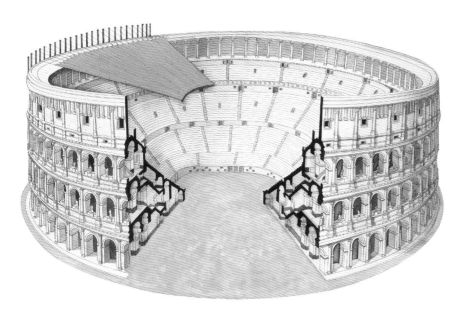

The Colosseum could seat tens of thousands of spectators.

Linus held his breath until he heard the sound again. This time it was louder—much louder. He was sure it was a very large animal.

Linus ran back down the dark passageway. He didn't know he could run so fast. He kept running until he saw a stairway. At the top of the stairway, he saw the sky.

A moment later, Linus was blinking at the bright sunlight in a sand-covered arena. He looked around. He was surrounded by fierce-looking warriors.

They were wearing helmets and carrying swords. They were covered with sweat and dust. They were looking at him.

Someone shouted, "Get that boy!"

Linus ran down the stairs and back into the dark passageway. He kept running.

Meanwhile, Lucia saw Nikos at the top of the Colosseum. He was delivering Grandfather's message to the naval commander.

A moment later, the great awning began to unroll. Lucia felt better. Soon the sailors would help find Linus, and she could stop worrying.

Suddenly, Linus ran through a doorway on the other side of the arena. He kept running until he reached his grandfather. He hugged him and would not let go. Linus was very pale.

"I'm glad you could join us, boy. We were just going to explore the underground chambers and visit the gladiator school." Grandfather teased.

Grandfather smiled and said, "Lucia, as much as I love this arena, I never come to the gladiator contests or the wild animal fights. I don't like killing, even though many Romans do. I'd rather watch the chariot races at the Circus Maximus."

Unlike many Romans, Grandfather did not like the wild animal fights.

"So would I, Grandfather," said Linus. "This place scares me. Could we leave here, please? Right now?"

"We will wait here for Nikos," said Grandfather. "While we are waiting, think of a special way to thank him for climbing to the top of the Colosseum to help find you. You will also tell your sister you are sorry."

Grandfather signaled to Nikos and pointed to Linus. Nikos spoke to the commander. The naval commander saluted the senator. Nikos started the long walk back down.

Circus Maximus and Chariot Races

On the way to the Circus Maximus, Nikos carried Linus on his shoulders, and Lucia held her grandfather's hand. It was a beautiful day, but the streets were almost empty.

"Where is everyone?" asked Lucia.

At that moment, a great roar filled the air. It was a lot like thunder. Another great roar sounded, even louder than the first one.

Grandfather laughed. "I'm certain that not everyone in Rome is in the Circus Maximus. But the Circus Maximus can seat 250,000 people. It is much larger than the Colosseum, with a huge oval racetrack. The chariot races are the most exciting show in Rome.

"They race twelve chariots, each pulled by four fast horses. The racetrack is a dangerous place. The drivers and the horses must be very well-trained. Even, so terrible accidents can happen."

Grandfather looked at Nikos. "Well, it's time to watch the races. Are you ready?"

Nikos was so excited he could hardly speak.

Chariot racing was considered good entertainment.

Chapter 13
Pompeii

Ruins The Romans were very good builders. Remains of their bridges, roads, aqueducts, and buildings are found in many places. A few ancient Roman bridges are still used today.

The Big Question

What do the ruins of Pompeii tell us about life in ancient Rome?

Vocabulary

ruin, n. what remains of an old building or structure

pollution, n. something that makes land, water, or air dirty and unsafe

The remains of many ancient buildings stand in Rome and other places. These remains are called **ruins**.

Roman ruins are thousands of years old. These old ruins are usually damaged.

Weather caused most of the damage. Heat, cold, rain, snow, hail, and wind all had an effect. Earthquakes and fires have caused problems, too.

People have also taken pieces from the ruins. Wars and air **pollution** have also had a harmful impact.

The ruins of many Roman buildings still stand today. These ruins of Pompeii, Italy, reveal a lot about the past.

It can be hard to picture what these buildings looked like in Roman times. However, there is an area in Italy where nature has **preserved** these ancient buildings. This area is southeast of Rome, near the Bay of Naples and Mount Vesuvius.

Mount Vesuvius

Mount Vesuvius is a **volcano**. A volcano is formed when melted, or molten, rock pushes up from deep underground.

Molten rock flows like mud. It pushes through cracks in **Earth's crust**. It then flows across earth's surface. Later it cools and becomes hard.

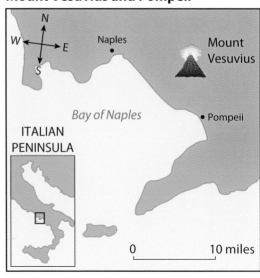

Vocabulary

preserve, v. to keep or save

volcano, n. a mountain that has cracks leading to openings deep inside the earth from which hot, melted rock may sometimes erupt

Earth's crust, n. the hard, thick outer layer of Earth's surface

debris, n. the pieces left over after something has been destroyed

Sometimes molten rock explodes out of a volcano. This is called a volcanic eruption. Rock and hot ash explode in the air and fall around the volcano. When this happens, plant and animal life are damaged or destroyed.

Sometimes smoke, dirt, and **debris** (/deh*bree/) from a volcanic eruption can block out the sun. The sky can stay dark for days as debris falls back to Earth.

Mount Vesuvius and Pompeii

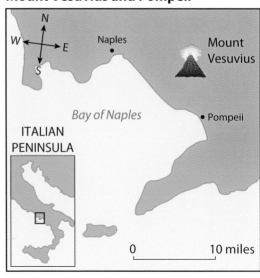

Mount Vesuvius is just a few miles from Pompeii.

Mount Vesuvius Buries Pompeii

Mount Vesuvius erupted on August 24, 79 CE. Rock and ash exploded from the volcano. The debris fell like rain for two days.

The town of Pompeii (/pom*pay/) was six miles away from Mount Vesuvius. Hot gas killed many people without warning. Then rock and ash from the eruption buried the town. Pompeii disappeared under twenty-three feet of volcanic debris.

The debris damaged every building in Pompeii. That same debris preserved Pompeii as it was at the moment the disaster struck. The town remained buried and forgotten for almost 1,700 years.

This painting shows what the eruption of Mount Vesuvius may have looked like.

Pompeii Is Found

The buried town was found in 1763. Since then, people from all over the world come to explore Pompeii. Some people come to search for statues or gold coins. Some people come to study Roman buildings. Others want to find out about volcanic eruptions. Everyone wants to know what happened on that awful day. It took years of digging to find certain answers.

Today, more than half of Pompeii has been dug up. This work is done by experts called **archaeologists**. They are still digging, slowly and carefully. While they want to find out more, they do not want to do any more harm to the ancient city's remains.

> **Vocabulary**
> ....
> **archaeologist,** n. an expert in the study of ancient people and the objects from their time period that remain
>
> **trade,** v. to buy and sell goods

Daily Life in Pompeii

Pompeii has taught us much about the Roman people. The buildings of Pompeii are filled with things people used every day. These things help us understand how ancient Romans lived.

Pompeii was a town of about twenty thousand people. The town was built next to a river. The river flowed into the Bay of Naples. Ships from all over the Roman world brought goods that could be **traded** in Pompeii.

The people of Pompeii traded wine, olive oil, grain, pottery, and wool cloth. In the busy marketplace, farmers sold fruits and vegetables. Politicians made speeches. Poets shared their latest poems.

The ruins of Pompeii, including this water fountain, give us a glimpse of daily life in Rome.

Pompeii had more than two hundred places to eat and drink. Craftspeople made and sold metal cups and dishes. Shops made and sold perfume. The town also had bakers, builders, and bankers.

The People of Pompeii

The people of Pompeii loved art. Paintings decorated the walls of shops and houses. Huge statues decorated the temples and the town forum. Beautiful **mosaics** decorated the walls and floors of houses and public buildings.

The people of Pompeii also had fun. They kept dogs and birds as pets. They built beautiful gardens. They bathed at the public baths or the town swimming pool. They wrestled at the town gym. The people of Pompeii watched plays and concerts in town theaters. They watched gladiators fight in the town **amphitheater**.

This room in a Pompeii house has a beautiful mosaic floor.

The people of Pompeii drank from public fountains. They wrote messages on the walls of almost every building. They built huge temples to their gods. Venus, the goddess of love, seems to have been their favorite.

We know all of these things because Mount Vesuvius erupted about two thousand years ago. The eruption was a disaster for the people of Pompeii. For historians, though, the eruption provided a helpful way to learn about life in the Roman world.

Chapter 14
The Romans and the Christians

Luciano Is Embarrassed It was the year 2016 in the city of Rome. The teacher looked around the classroom and began the lesson: "After he defeated Antony and Cleopatra, Octavian was the ruler of the Roman world."

The Big Question

Why was Christianity considered to be dangerous to Rome?

The teacher continued: "Octavian allowed the Senate to name him Augustus. He also liked the titles 'First Citizen of Rome' and 'Father of Rome.' He never allowed the Senate to name him king. But it did not matter. The Roman Republic was gone forever.

"Augustus was the first Roman emperor, even though he never admitted it. Emperors ruled in Rome for the next five hundred years. They ruled in Constantinople for one thousand years after that."

The teacher turned to one of the students. "Luciano, who was Octavian?" All the students turned to look at Luciano (/loo*chee*ah*noe/).

"I'm sorry," Luciano said. "I wasn't listening. I was looking through the window." Luciano was very embarrassed.

Statue of Caesar Augustus, the first Roman emperor

"I accept your apology, Luciano. You are honest. But I don't want your apology. I want you to learn. Come up here near me and take a seat." Luciano picked up his things and quickly moved to his new seat.

"Tonight I want everyone to read about the early Roman emperors who followed Augustus. Tomorrow we will talk about them. Luciano, please stay. The rest of you may go home now."

Homework for Luciano

When the other students had gone, the teacher spoke to Luciano. "Today was your last day looking through the window during class. Tomorrow is your first day as a student." The teacher smiled as Luciano sighed.

The teacher continued, "You will tell the class about the years of the great Roman peace, the *Pax Romana*. Your homework is to read about this time in the early days of the Roman Empire."

Luciano thought about his task as he walked home. The streets of Rome were crowded and noisy. He wondered if Rome had been this crowded during the time of emperors.

When Luciano got home, he began learning about the great Roman peace. He was still reading when his brother called him to dinner.

The Great Roman Peace

The next day, Luciano took his seat in the classroom. The teacher told the class, "Luciano is going to tell us about the great Roman peace. Please listen carefully."

Luciano stood up. "For the first two hundred years after Augustus, the Roman empire was mostly peaceful," he said. "The people of the Roman world were safe from civil war. The empire grew larger and wealthier than ever before.

"During this time, most of the emperors were wise and generous. Only a few were mean and selfish," he said.

"Thank you, Luciano. You have done well," said the teacher. Luciano was happy. He enjoyed reading about the history of his city. After school, the teacher said, "Tomorrow, you will tell us about the early Christians who lived during this time."

The Early Christians

The next day Luciano shared what he had learned.

"The early Christians were people who followed the teachings of Jesus. They believed in one God. They also believed it was most important to live in God's kingdom after they died. The Romans did not like the idea of any kingdom being more important than Rome.

"The Christians respected the government and paid their taxes. Still, many Romans thought the Christians were dangerous to Rome. The Romans were always afraid of angering the gods. They wanted everyone in the empire to worship their own gods *and* the Roman gods too. This way, the Romans thought, no gods would get angry and punish the Romans.

"The Romans thought that the Christians were careless. The Christians worshiped only one God. They would not worship the

Roman gods. The Romans thought the Christians might anger the other gods. Then the whole human race would be in trouble."

Persecution

The teacher smiled brightly. "Thank you, Luciano. You did a fine job again today."

The teacher turned to the class. "The Romans **persecuted** the Christians because of their **religious beliefs**. Whenever something bad happened in Rome, the Romans blamed the Christians.

According to legend, Nero played music while Rome burned around him.

88

"For example, there was a terrible fire in 64 CE. Large areas of Rome were destroyed. The emperor Nero blamed the Christians. Nero was a selfish man, though. According to legend, he cared so little about Rome that he played a musical instrument called a lyre while the city burned. Today we have an expression, 'fiddling while Rome burns.' It means paying no attention to great disasters happening around you.

"At times the Christians were treated as criminals. They were put in prison or killed. Sometimes Christians were made to face wild animals in the Colosseum.

"The Romans persecuted the Christians for many years. It was dangerous to be a Christian. Still, the number of Christians continued to grow. This is because the Christians welcomed poor people and enslaved people. Christians promised a better life in the next world, after death. This was appealing to those who suffered in the Roman world."

Some Christians were killed in public arenas such as the Colosseum. Romans, including the emperor, considered this a form of entertainment.

Chapter 15
The Decline of the Roman Empire

Luciano's Next Assignment Luciano enjoyed taking part in class. Each day the teacher gave him a special assignment. The next day, Luciano would tell the class what he had learned.

The Big Question

What did Diocletian do to help prevent the total collapse of the Roman Empire?

Vocabulary

assignment, n. a task or job given to someone

decline, v. to grow weaker

Luciano thought about his latest **assignment** as he walked home from school. The teacher told him to read about the time after the great Roman peace. During that time, the empire began to **decline**. Luciano wondered what had happened.

As he walked, Luciano crossed a beautiful old stone bridge. He knew the ancient Romans built the bridge. Millions of people had used the bridge in the many years since then. Luciano was proud to be a Roman.

When he got home, Luciano told his mother about his assignment. She was pleased. She wanted him to work hard and enjoy learning.

Luciano sat down to read. His teacher said there had been big changes.

A graceful Roman bridge shows the city's glorious past.

Weak and Corrupt Emperors

The next day, Luciano told the class how Rome changed. "The honorable emperors of the great Roman peace were gone. For the next fifty years, most of the emperors faced many problems. For example, Rome suffered attacks from outsiders, civil war, and widespread illness. Some emperors were too weak to solve these problems. Others, such as Nero, ignored the people's needs. They looked after only themselves."

The teacher stood up. "That is correct, Luciano. Many emperors were too weak or too selfish to serve the people well. They could not protect the provinces from attack. Protecting the provinces cost a lot of money.

"Some **corrupt** emperors named greedy men to be generals in the army. Sometimes a general would kill the emperor. Then that general would become the new emperor.

> **Vocabulary**
>
> **corrupt,** adj. having done something dishonest for personal gain

"The new emperor would then kill the family and friends of the old emperor. Sometimes there were two or three emperors in one year. Many powerful Romans were killed. For the old patrician families, life during this time could be very dangerous.

"Sometimes generals fought each other to take over the empire.

Some Roman families were forced to leave their homes.

The fighting destroyed many towns and farms. These civil wars also made trading difficult. In some places, people had very little food. People lost their jobs and their homes. Throughout the empire, people often lived in fear."

The Barbarians Invade

The teacher turned back to Luciano. "What other changes happened during this time?"

Luciano said, "The Roman army was also very different. There were many soldiers who no longer fought for the glory of Rome. Many of these soldiers came from Roman territories that were far from Rome itself. The Romans called these outsiders *barbarians*. The Romans thought the barbarians

The barbarians invaded Roman lands.

were uncivilized. That is, they did not know the rules of being a good citizen. Still, the Romans needed them to serve in the Roman army."

"Very good, Luciano," the teacher said. "Those were important changes in the Roman army. Many barbarians lived along the borders of the Roman Empire. Sometimes large armies of certain barbarian groups invaded Roman provinces."

"Sometimes Rome's armies had to fight barbarian invaders and a civil war at the same time. Many of Rome's best soldiers died fighting other Romans."

Rome's Army Grows Weak

"During this time, Rome's leaders treated the army badly. Soldiers sometimes had to wait for months or even years to get paid.

Barbarian attacks almost made the Roman Empire collapse.

Without money to buy food, the soldiers stole food to live. Many Roman soldiers lived by **pillaging** nearby farms and towns.

"Over time, the Roman army became weak and dishonest, like the Roman government.

> **Vocabulary**
>
> **pillage,** v. to steal things using force
>
> **collapse,** v. to fail or end suddenly

"Meanwhile, the barbarian armies grew stronger. They forced the Romans out of large areas in the western and northern parts of the empire. Eventually, the Roman Empire was ready to **collapse**."

Diocletian

The teacher continued: "Then a strong, thoughtful man named Diocletian (/dye*oe*klee*shun/) became emperor. He defeated a fierce barbarian army. Luciano, can you tell us what else Diocletian did?"

Luciano jumped to his feet. He spoke in a clear voice. "Diocletian changed the whole Roman government. He divided the empire into two parts with two emperors. One emperor governed the western part. Another governed the eastern part. Diocletian named honest, hardworking men to

This coin shows the emperor Diocletian wearing a laurel wreath. He ruled from 284 to 305 CE.

rule the empire with him. After he ruled for twenty years, he did something no emperor had ever done. He gave up his job."

Chapter 16
East and West

Luciano's Last Assignment Luciano glanced ahead in his books. He knew the story of the Roman Empire was nearly over. He felt a little sad because this story was special to him.

The Big Question

Why did the Western Empire collapse, but the Eastern Empire survive for much longer?

While studying the Roman Empire, Luciano discovered he liked taking part in class.

For his next assignment, the teacher told him to read about Emperor Constantine and the city of Constantinople. Luciano was curious. He hurried home to begin his studies.

Constantine Takes Control

The next day, the teacher told the class about Constantine. "After Diocletian retired, the Roman Empire fell into civil war. In time, a strong leader took control of the empire. His name was Constantine.

This mosaic shows Constantine holding a model of Constantinople.

A key victory in Constantine's rise to power came in 312 CE. At the Battle of the Milvian Bridge, Constantine defeated one of his rivals. Constantine was not yet a Christian. But he claimed the Christian God helped him win the battle.

"In 313 CE, Constantine made an agreement with Licinius, who then ruled the eastern part of the empire. The two agreed to let Christians **practice** their religion. This agreement was called the Edict of Milan. Christians were no longer punished for their beliefs. In fact, Constantine actively supported the Christian religion. He is remembered as the first Christian emperor.

Vocabulary

practice, v. to live according to the teachings of a religion or other set of ideas

"Constantine was a strong emperor. He followed Diocletian's example. He named honest people to help him rule. After Constantine ruled the Roman Empire for a while, he moved the government away from Rome."

The teacher turned to Luciano. "Luciano, where did Constantine move the government?"

Constantinople

Luciano was prepared. "In 324 CE, Constantine began moving the government of the Roman Empire to Byzantium. Byzantium was an old city in the eastern part of the empire. It had a big racetrack like Rome's Circus Maximus.

"Constantine thought that Byzantium should have a new name. He named the city Constantinople after himself.

"You won't find Constantinople on maps today," Luciano continued. "The city's name has changed. Today it's called Istanbul, and it's in the country of Turkey."

"Thank you, Luciano," said the teacher. "You did well."

The Byzantine Empire

The teacher continued: "Constantine ruled from Constantinople for several years. After his death, there were more civil wars. The western part of the Roman Empire eventually broke away from the eastern part. There were now two empires instead of one.

Eastern and Western Roman Empires, 330 CE

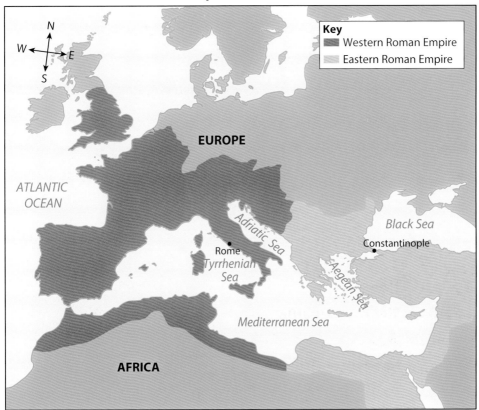

After the division of the Roman Empire, Constantinople became the capital of the east.

"The Eastern Empire included Constantinople. Because the city was once called Byzantium, the empire was called the Byzantine Empire. The Byzantine Empire became powerful and lasted for more than one thousand years.

"Constantinople became one of the most important cities in the world. It attracted traders and travelers from Asia, Africa, and Europe. Byzantine philosophers talked about important ideas. Artists blended Greek, Roman, and Middle Eastern styles to create beautiful mosaics and other works of art.

"The Eastern Empire was ruled by a series of emperors. Justinian was one of its most famous emperors. In Constantinople, Justinian built a beautiful Christian church called Hagia Sophia (/hah*jah/ soe*fee*uh/).

The emperor Justinian had a Christian church called Hagia Sophia built in Constantinople, which is now called Istanbul.

"Although Justinian ruled the Eastern Empire, far from Rome, he knew the Romans had built his empire. The empire was governed by Roman laws. Justinian had these Roman laws written down. This collection of laws was known as the Justinian Code."

The Western Empire

The teacher continued: "The Western Empire was not as strong as the Eastern Empire. By the time Justinian became emperor in the East, the Western Empire had collapsed.

"How did this happen? The Western Empire was less wealthy than the Eastern Empire. It was also surrounded by warlike neighbors. Barbarians often attacked the borders of the Western Empire. Over time, these barbarians took over more and more Roman land. The armies of the Western Empire could not stop them. Eventually the barbarians **sacked** the city of Rome.

> **Vocabulary**
>
> **sack,** v. to steal and destroy things in a city that has been defeated by an army

"The Western Empire kept fighting the barbarians for another sixty years. Finally, in 476 CE, the emperor of the Western Empire surrendered to a barbarian leader. The Western Empire had fallen. This event is called the fall of Rome.

"We have reached the end of our exploration of ancient Rome," said the teacher. "We should thank Luciano for helping us to know and understand the Romans. Thank you, Luciano. We are proud of you."

Glossary

A

amphitheater, n. an outdoor round or oval building that has an open space surrounded by rising rows of seats (82)

aqueduct, n. a structure for carrying water across long distances (47)

arch, n. a curved structure that has an opening below and that supports something above (60)

archaeologist, n. an expert in the study of ancient people and the objects from their time period that remain (80)

arena, n. an area surrounded by seating for the public, where sports events are held (70)

assassinate, v. to kill a ruler or member of the government (40)

assembly, n. a group of people that makes laws (18)

assignment, n. a task or job given to someone (90)

B

barge, n. a boat with a flat bottom, usually used for carrying goods (36)

barrier, n. something that is in the way (26)

border, n. an imaginary line that marks the edge of a country or other piece of land (32)

C

capital, n. the main city of a country and the home of the country's government (2)

chamber, n. a small space or room (70)

charcoal, n. black chunks made from burned wood that are used as a fuel (12)

chariot, n. a carriage with two wheels that was pulled by horses or other animals (16)

citizen, n. a person who belongs to a country and has protections under that country's laws (17)

civil war, n. a war between people who live in the same country (33)

collapse, v. to fail or end suddenly (95)

Colosseum, n. a large stadium in ancient Rome (68)

conquer, v. to win control of a land and its people by attacking an enemy or fighting a war (22)

consul, n. the most important official in the Roman Republic (19)

continent, n. one of the seven large land areas on Earth (50)

corrupt, adj. having done something dishonest for personal gain (92)

D

debris, n. the pieces left over after something has been destroyed (78)

decline, v. to grow weaker (90)

descendant, n. someone who is related to a person or group of people who lived in the past (37)

dictator, n. a ruler who has total control over the country (19)

E

Earth's crust, n. the hard, thick outer layer of Earth's surface (78)

ember, n. a small piece of burning wood or coal from a dying fire (12)

emperor, n. the ruler of an empire (49)

empire, n. a group of countries or territories under the control of one government or one ruler (42)

F

foreigner, n. someone from another country (42)

formation, n. an orderly arrangement, such as in rows or a line (24)

Forum, n. the area in the center of Rome where government buildings, temples, and other important monuments were built (19)

G

gladiator, n. a man in ancient Rome who fought another man or an animal to entertain the public (64)

god, n. a being in the shape of a man who has the power to affect nature or people's lives (8)

goddess, n. a being in the shape of a woman who has the power to affect nature or people's lives (10)

governor, n. the leader of the government in a province (28)

gravel, n. tiny stones used to make paths or to make concrete (59)

H

holy, adj. having to do with a god or religion (10)

K

king, n. a male ruler who comes to power by birth and who rules for life (6)

kingdom, n. a country ruled by a king or queen (54)

L

legend, n. an old, well-known story, usually more entertaining than truthful (2)

M

marble, n. a kind of stone that is used in buildings and sculptures (65)

mosaic, n. artwork made of many small pieces of colorful stone or tile (82)

mountain range, n. a line of mountains (52)

N

nation, n. the land and people who live under the authority of a government and its laws; a country (22)

noble, adj. belonging to the highest social class (43)

P

patrician, n. a member of ancient Rome's highest social class; a wealthy landowner in ancient Rome (17)

patron, n. a person who gives money or other support to someone, such as an artist (49)

peninsula, n. a piece of land sticking out into a body of water, so that it is almost surrounded by water (22)

persecute, v. to treat people cruelly and unfairly (88)

pillage, v. to steal things using force (95)

pillar, n. a tall, solid support post (60)

plebeian, n. a common person without power in ancient Rome (17)

pollution, n. something that makes land, water, or air dirty and unsafe (76)

practice, v. to live according to the teachings of a religion or other set of ideas (98)

preserve, v. to keep or save (78)

province, n. an area or region; when an area was conquered by Rome, it became a province under Roman control (28)

R

"religious belief," (phrase), an idea about gods or faith that someone accepts as true (88)

"religious ceremony," (phrase), a formal event to honor a god or goddess (48)

representative, n. a person who speaks or acts for someone else (6)

republic, n. a kind of government where people elect representatives to rule for them (17)

ruin, n. what remains of an old building or structure (76)

S

sack, v. to steal and destroy things in a city that has been defeated by an army (101)

sacred, adj. related to religion; holy (11)

scroll, n. a roll of paper or other material with written information (56)

Senate, n. the patrician lawmaking group in ancient Rome; the most powerful group in the Roman Republic (18)

senator, n. a member of the Senate, the patrician lawmaking group in ancient Rome (17)

stake, n. a thin pointed post (60)

strait, n. a narrow body of water that connects two large bodies of water (53)

supplies, n. food and other goods that are needed for a certain purpose (43)

surface, n. the top layer (59)

symbol, n. a picture or object that is a sign for something; for example, the American flag is a symbol of the United States (12)

T

tax, n. money that people pay to the government (28)

temple, n. a building used for worship (11)

toga, n. a robe-like piece of clothing worn in ancient Rome (40)

trade, v. to buy and sell goods (80)

V

valley, n. a low area of land surrounded by higher ground, such as hills or mountains (60)

volcano, n. a mountain that has cracks leading to openings deep inside the earth from which hot, melted rock may sometimes erupt (78)

Core Knowledge®

CKHG™
Core Knowledge HISTORY AND GEOGRAPHY™

Series Editor-In-Chief
E.D. Hirsch, Jr.

Editorial Directors
Linda Bevilacqua and Rosie McCormick

Subject Matter Expert

Michael J. Carter, PhD, Professor, Department of Classics, Brock University

Illustration and Photo Credits